Foreword by Dale Mast

Handfuls of Purpose

Prophetic Gleanings from the Fields of Life

By Bill Yount

Bill Yount

Handfuls of Purpose
Prophetic Gleanings from the Fields of Life
Copyright © 2018 by Bill C. Yount

Published by
Blowing the Shofar Ministries
132 E. North Ave.
Hagerstown, MD 21740
www.billyount.com

Bill Yount

ISBN-13: 978-1724516336
ISBN-10: 1724516337

Printed in the United States of America
For Worldwide Distribution

Cover Design by Justin Heinen

Endorsements

"Bill Yount is a God-called seer prophet who has totally yielded himself to the Lord's forge validating for us his gifts of powerful life nuggets. He's a prophetic voice balanced with wisdom and love. I heartily endorse Bill's book, *"Handfuls of Purpose-Prophetic Gleanings from the Fields of Life,"* as a handbook to receive very real prophetic life applications that will raise your understanding of God's purpose in your calling and destiny."

John Mark Pool
Co-founder of *Word to the World Ministries* and author of *"Path of a Prophet"* and *'Love, God's Greatest Gift."*
www.w2wmin.org

"'Prophetic gleanings' are when we acquire what others miss. *Handfuls of Purpose* reveals the current condition of the Body of Christ and the challenges it faces. This is something Christians need to glean. Over the 30 years I have known Bill Yount, his insightful revelations have always been pertinent, beneficial and timely. *"A word spoken in due season, how good it is!"* Proverbs 15:23 (KJV) This book is exactly that."

Randy Walter
Shiloh Ministries
Co-author with his wife Barbara of *Name Your Gates & Take Back Your Cities* plus 10 other books.

"In his innovative, creative style, Bill Yount has once again compiled a volume of his prophetic writings; this time around the theme of life purpose. You will be encouraged and strengthened in your calling through Bill's unique ability to use vivid imagery and parables from everyday life to express the words he receives from the Lord. Pick up a copy and read, ponder, and pray into each word. Your life will be enriched!"

Diane M. Fink
Author, Speaker, Prophetic Minister with a heart for the Middle East
Twitter: @DianeFink218

"An encourager with a unique prophetic gift, Bill Yount has a special anointing that inspires many to rise and shine in the midst of great challenges and adversity. "I love it!" Full of directive and encouraging words that bring hope. I can't think of anything more needed in the times we are living in. I urge you to open the pages of this book and glean from the fields of life."

Ruth Willard,
Founder of *KEY Fellowship*
keyfellowship@verizon.net
www.keyfellowship.com

Table of Contents

Foreword

Bill Yount has a distinctive prophetic gift that brings life. This book, *Handfuls of Purpose*, is filled with hope, faith and revelation. As you read the different prophetic words let it open up your heart towards heaven and receive a fresh anointing. His prophetic words often start with a mystery and finish with refreshing revelation. The simplicity and anointing in his words are life-changing.

My wife opened up one of his prophetic words concerning the end-time revival and family. We prayed with increased faith over our family with the prophetic word he shared. This book will help you fight the good fight of faith.

"This charge I commit to you, son Timothy, according to the prophecies previously made concerning you, that by them you may wage the good warfare..." 1 Timothy 1:18 NKJV

This is not just a book to read, but a book to read and pray. Many victories will be obtained if you will step up in faith to the prophetic words given. I know that many of you will receive miracles as you read this book and pray. Enjoy!

Dale L. Mast
Prophet and Pastor
Author: *And David Perceived He Was King, Two Sons And A Father, The Throne Of David*

Bill Yount

Acknowledgements

Thanks to my beautiful wife, Dagmar, who is a pillar of strength and love that keeps me going forward in a world that's going backwards. Gleaning together in the home field is the most important field there is.

Thank you Lord, for the field of life where I always find purpose as I glean from your love and faithfulness. For the seven years in the steel mill where your call came to me: "Lay down your nets and follow Me."

I thank you for the twenty - three years of Prison Ministry at Mount Hope Inc. in Hagerstown, Maryland where I gleaned from inmates much more than they gleaned from me.

Thank you, *Bridge of Life*, my home church, for your love and support going on forty years now. And for Pastor Terry King who taught me that we never stop growing.

Thank you, Cheryl Jenkins, Founder of *Kingdom One Business Solutions,* who has given oversight to my last three books and makes me look like I know what I'm doing. And for Betsy Elliot who proof reads and gives me joyful encouragement.

I am honored by the covering of the *Apostolic Company of Alliance International Ministries* for their encouragement and instruction in helping me to keep putting one foot in front of the other.

I am thankful for the online ministries of Spirit Fuel, Charisma, and The Elijah List who have posted my writings to reach so many people.

Thank you to everyone who prays for my family and ministry. Your prayers are keeping us in the field of harvest. We love you all.

Introduction

Handfuls of purpose. Isn't that what we all want? Hands that are full with purpose, and not just with any old purpose, but with God's purpose.

Bill Yount is one servant who has spent years gleaning in the field of God's word and has reaped a harvest, resulting in hands full of His purpose. This humble servant has shared His gleanings with many hearts through delivering live sermons, posting prophetic words online and even through blasts of the shofar! I am humbled and honored to write the introduction for Bill's latest book, a collection of the cream of the crop that He so graciously is sharing with us!

Our hands only become full of purpose when we first purpose in our hearts to serve Jehovah. We see this beautifully illustrated in the book of Ruth. Ruth was a Moabitess, an outcast, a widow who purposed in her heart to follow and serve the one true living God, the God of Abraham, Isaac and Jacob. As Ruth humbled herself with empty hands before the Lord, He began to fill them with His purposes.

After leaving her homeland and the gods of her fathers, Ruth clung to her mother-in-law, Naomi, and traveled to Bethlehem in the land of Judah. There in "The House of Bread", Ruth began to glean the corners of a barley field, as widows were instructed in the Torah. Ruth "happened" upon the field of Boaz, who is a shadow of Jesus. Boaz, a wealthy landowner, noticed Ruth and told her to remain in his field and not to glean elsewhere. He also offered her fresh-drawn water while she worked and invited her to enjoy bread and wine at his table for dinner. As a despised foreigner from Moab, Ruth could not understand Boaz's kindness. However, Boaz had heard of her faithfulness to her mother-in-law, Naomi and ultimately her faithfulness to God.

Boaz continued to lavish his favor on Ruth by commanding his servants not to touch her and to allow her to glean, not just from the corners of his field, but from the sheaves themselves. Boaz's extravagant provision and protection of Ruth is further expressed as he declares these words to his servants concerning Ruth. *"And let fall also some of the **handfuls of purpose** for her, and leave them, that she may glean them, and rebuke her not."* Ruth 2:16 (KJV)

The expression "handfuls of purpose" in Hebrew translates: "tsebeth" - a bundle of grain, a handful... and "shalal"- to drop on purpose as spoil or plunder. This Hebrew translation speaks volumes of the Lord's great love toward us as we choose Him as Father. As we purpose in our hearts to follow Abba and glean in His field, He purposes in His heart to bless us with protection, provision and plunder--- and on purpose... for His purposes! What a mighty God we serve! This scripture rises up in my heart... "See what great love the Father has lavished on us, that we should be called children of God!" 1 John 3:1 (NIV)

As you turn through the pages of *"Handfuls of Purpose"* expect to taste and see that the Lord is good! The Lord has given Bill the ability to share His truth with humility and humor and to deliver the word in the perfect dosage. You will notice the format of this book is designed to serve you with a quick kernel of encouragement or offer you a longer word to chew on as you navigate the field of life. May you feast on the plunder, provision, and lavish extravagance from the Lord's field.

It is Bill's delight and calling to encourage the Body of Christ to move forward into God's destiny as they are sent into the harvest field. That is the purpose of this book! It is not an accident this book is in your hands. It is here in your hands on purpose designed to encourage you in His purpose for your life. May you feast on these prophetic gleanings and not give up nor fail to gather the seed of His word, for you will reap a harvest and bring in sheaves of blessings as you do! So a-gleaning we go!

"Let us not become weary in doing good, for at the proper time we will reap a harvest if we do not give up." Gal 6:9 (NIV)

"Those who sow in tears shall reap with joyful shouting. He who goes to and fro weeping, carrying his bag of seed, Shall indeed come again with a shout of joy, bringing his sheaves with him". Psalm 126:5-6 (NASB)

"And He was saying, "The kingdom of God is like a man who casts seed upon the soil and he goes to bed at night and gets up by day, and the seed sprouts and grows—how, he himself does not know. The soil produces crops by itself; first the blade, then the head, then the mature grain in the head. But when the crop permits, he immediately puts in the sickle,

because the harvest has come." Mark 4:26-29 (NASB)

Christine Vales
Author & Teacher of "*His Appointed Times"*
Uncovering the Lord's Prophetic Timepiece in Real-Time
www.christinevales.com

Section One

Empty Hands Serve a Purpose

"Don't miss your crucifixion."

A Stump in The Field

I saw the Body of Christ plowing with great difficulty in the field of labor. Finally, our plow seemed to hit a stump in the field and we couldn't go any further. With all our efforts and praying, this stump remained unmovable and steadfast. Our hearts were broken for we knew God had placed us here to plow in this great field of Harvest. But this 'stump' in the field was stopping us.

You Have Hit Treasure

I then heard the Lord say, "You have hit treasure! This is no ordinary stump or ordinary tree. You have just hit the base of the tree of Calvary. It's the cross growing in your field! You must not, I repeat, you must not remove it. It is growing in your field to remove you out of the way from hindering My Harvest. You will have to embrace this cross and die before I can release resurrection power into your field of labor.

As I beheld the cross growing in our field, we began to experience a "Severe Pruning" in our spiritual giftings, especially in the area of the prophetic. He was cutting and pruning us back to bring forth a more, sure word. He was adjusting our gifts, callings, and ministries to bring forth the fruit of "Servant Hood" in our lives. I heard the Lord say, "Your giftings are showing more than your fruit. You are embarrassing Me!"

There Are Times You Don't Prophesy

I then remembered right before the cross-- they beat on Jesus and cried out to Him – "Prophesy to us!" but He didn't.... there are times you don't prophesy - you just show others how to die - to self, giftings and plans.

As we embrace the cross, death and surrender will bring forth fruit that will remain to bring in the Harvest. In fact, fruit is the Harvest - it will bring it in. In Italy they have discovered that grape vines produce more fruit when grown on cross-like poles. They get more sunshine and fresh air.

Go 'This Way' =|= Spread Out Your Arms, You are at the Cross

Many are spiritually "stumped" in their lives, families and ministries this hour. They feel they are at a cross-roads and are looking for a fresh word from heaven to tell them what to do. Many are asking, "Lord, should I go this way or that way?" But I sense the Lord saying, "Go this way =|= spread out your arms.

You are NOT at a crossroads, you ARE at the cross!" Have you been betrayed? You are nearing your cross.

Have you been rejected? You are getting closer. Don't run now. If you miss your crucifixion - you will miss your resurrection!

"And when he had called the people unto him with his disciples also, he said unto them, Whosoever will come after me, let him deny himself, and take up his cross, and follow me." Mark 8:34 (KJV)

No Crushing, No Anointing!

Forty years have taught me: A fresh anointing is preceded by a great crushing. That's just the way it works. Welcome to the Kingdom of God!

"Anyone who falls on this stone will be broken to pieces; anyone on whom it falls will be crushed." Matthew 21:44 (NIV)

Some Miracles Begin in Mud

One day Jesus picked up some earth and spit on it and made mud. He touched the eyes of a blind man with it - and the blind man saw! How many of us today would get in that prayer line?

Naaman was told to go dip in the muddy Jordan River to get healed! He came up a "muddy healed" man! One disciple asked Jesus, "Why did you use mud?" This question was best answered at a theatre production I attended of Jesus when He answered, "Most people's lives have to get messy before they get better." Where you see mud, God can do a miracle.

"After saying this, he (Jesus) spit on the ground, made some mud with the saliva, and put it on the man's eyes." John 9:6 (NIV)

Section Two

Gleaning in the Fields of Life

Bill Yount

"Don't be

a fish

out of

water."

26

Many Seeds Were Shouting, "Our Season of Death Is Over!"

In the Spirit I am hearing a sound that I have never heard before. It's a sound from seeds that God has planted through us that have died inside the stony hearts of many people. It has been a long season and these seeds were not heard from at all. They were silenced by death. But in spite of death, these seeds now were beginning to groan as though death itself could no longer keep them.

The very life of Christ within these seeds was now beginning to overcome death and I saw a sprouting taking place that began to shake the gates of Hell off its hinges. It's as though these seeds were shouting, "Our season of death is over. We are now coming alive!" Seeds that had died with unfulfilled dreams of God inside of them were now breaking forth, worshiping their Creator, as they were beginning to sprout.

I am learning that when I feel like fainting, that is when I'm actually doing well from God's point of view, and a seed that I've sown is beginning to groan and sprout somewhere, in some place, or in somebody, or in some nation.

"Very truly I tell you, unless a kernel of wheat falls to the ground and dies, it remains only a

single seed. But if it dies, it produces many seeds. John 12:24 (NIV)

God is Not Through Writing Your Story

For some reason the Lord allows drama in our lives. I start more books than I finish. The ones I finish are the ones that adversity strikes in about the 9th or 10th chapter. The adversity keeps me reading to see how things are going to turn out. I sense many of your lives are in about the 10th chapter, but it doesn't end there. God's not through writing your story.

"You yourselves are our letter, written on our hearts, known and read by everyone." 2 Corinthians 3:2 (NIV)

I Have Learned to Swim by Sinking

We are all made out of the same stuff... dust. At times we feel like we are being blown away by life's situations. If you have never experienced this, check your pulse.

When I feel like quitting and question my purpose, I keep going on anyway and somehow encouragement pops up somewhere and keeps my head above water. Then as I keep moving forward, in spite of my feelings, more encouragement comes out of nowhere and then all of sudden I find myself walking on water!

Please don't isolate yourself. Force yourself to go to church or some fellowship. I have learned to swim by sinking. Don't be a fish out of water.

"...not giving up meeting together, as some are in the habit of doing, but encouraging one another—and all the more as you see the Day approaching."
Hebrews 10:25 (NIV)

Trust God's Faithfulness to You

About fifteen years ago I was in the hospital with a blood clot in the artery of my heart. I was given a fifty-fifty chance of living. I was flooded with thoughts like; where did I fail? What did I do to bring this upon me? As I began thinking, my mind was flooded with failures, like where did I blow it this time?

A mature sister in the Lord walked into my hospital room not knowing the battle going on in my mind. She said, "Bill, I sense strongly that I am to tell you that now is not the time to wonder about your faithfulness to the Lord, but to trust in His faithfulness to you. It's not about your faithfulness to Him; it's about His faithfulness to you." Because of God's faithfulness I'm still here! I believe this will be a year of God's great faithfulness. God's great faithfulness will override doubt, unbelief, failures and will heal and restore many. His goodness will lead many to repentance. There will be many testimonies: *"Great is Thy Faithfulness, Lord, unto me."*[1]

---

[1] Chisholm, Thomas O., Great is Thy Faithfulness, 1923; Copyright 1923, renewed 1951 by Hope Publishing

"Because of the Lord's great love we are not consumed, for his compassions never fail. They are new every morning; great is your faithfulness."
Lamentations 3:22-23 (KJV)

Billy Graham Never Forgot the Cows

It's well known that Billy Graham started out by preaching to cows and tree stumps. It's those hidden ones who have been practicing their sermons in cornfields, preaching to the ears of corn and in the woods, seeing trees as men walking, who will now be called upon to minister on city sidewalks and in stadiums across the earth. The earth will be their pulpit. When God raises you up, don't forget the cornfields and woods. Billy Graham never did.

"And Samuel said, When thou wast little in thine own sight, wast thou not made the head of the tribes of Israel, and the Lord anointed thee king over Israel?"
Samuel 15:17 (KJV)

"Out of these

prisons will

come forth

an army."

Billy Graham's Mantle Fell on Prisons Worldwide

I heard the Father saying, "I am honoring the inmates who built the casket for My chosen servant, Billy Graham. Their names burned into the pine, plywood casket represent a list of names without number that will be recorded in My Lamb's Book of Life. As Billy Graham's mantle falls on prisoners worldwide, including those held captive in spiritual prisons, and those who have been kept by the darkest bondages will now become the greatest evangelists of our day."

This is a word for those in a physical and/or spiritual prison. Whether you are inside a physical prison or a spiritual one, it makes no difference to the Lord!

I believe this word is the fruition of a vision the Lord gave me back in 1997:

God's Treasures Locked Up Behind Bars and Razor Wire

It was late, I was tired and wanted to go to sleep, but God wanted to talk to me. It was about midnight, but it dawned on me that God does not sleep. His question made me restless, "Bill, where on earth does man keep his most priceless treasures and valuables?"

I said, "Lord, usually these treasures like gold, silver,

diamonds and precious jewels are kept locked up somewhere out of sight, and usually with guards and security to keep them under lock and key."

God spoke, "Like man, My most valuable treasures on earth are also locked up."

I then saw Jesus standing in front of seemingly thousands of prisons and jails. The Lord said, "These ones have almost been destroyed by the enemy, but they have the greatest potential to be used and to bring forth glory to My name.

Tell My people, I am going this hour to the prisons to activate the gifts and callings that lie dormant in these lives, which were given before the foundation of the earth. Out from these walls will come forth an army of spiritual giants. They will have power to literally kick down the gates of Hell and overcome satanic powers that are holding many of My own people bound in My own house."

Tell My people that great treasures are behind these walls in these forgotten vessels. My people must come forth and touch these ones, for a mighty anointing will be unleashed upon them for future victory in My Kingdom. They must be restored."

I then saw the Lord step up to the prison doors with a key. One key fit every lock, and the gates began to open. I then heard and saw great explosions which sounded like dynamite going off behind the walls. It sounded like all-out spiritual warfare.

Jesus turned and said, "Tell My people to go in now and pick up the spoil and rescue these." Jesus then began walking in and touching inmates who were thronging Him. Many who were touched instantly had a golden glow come over them."

God spoke to me, "There's the gold!" Others had a silver glow around them. God said, "There's the silver!"

"Now Go and Pull Down Those Strongholds!"

As if in slow motion, these people began to grow into what appeared to be giant knights wearing warrior's armor. They had on the entire armor of God, and every piece was solid and pure gold, even golden shields. When I saw the golden shields, I heard the Lord say to these warriors: "Now, go and take what satan has taught you and use it all against him. Go and pull down the strongholds coming against My Church."

These spiritual giants then started stepping over the prison walls (spiritually), and they went immediately to the front line to battle with the enemy. I saw these unknown warriors surpass some big name ministers, as they walked by them to the battle line like David going after Goliath. They crossed the enemy's line and started delivering many of God's people from the clutches of satan, while demons trembled and fled out of sight at their presence.

Who Are These People?

No one, not even the Church, seemed to know who these spiritual giants were or where they came from. All you could see was their armor (the golden armor of God), from head to foot, and their shields of gold.

I also saw silver, precious treasures and vessels being brought in. Beneath the gold and silver were the people nobody knew: rejects of society, street people, the outcasts, the poor and the despised. These were the treasures that were missing from God's house. The shields were restored to God's house, and there was great victory and rejoicing.

In closing, the Lord said, "If My people want to know where they are needed, tell them they are needed in the streets, the hospitals, the missions and prisons. When they go there, they will find Me and the next move of My Spirit. They will be judged by My Word in Matthew 25:42-43 (KJV): *"For I was hungry and you gave Me no food, I was thirsty and you gave Me no drink, I was a stranger and you did not take Me in, I was naked and you did not clothe Me, I was sick and in prison and you did not visit Me."*

tangible, physical needs
+ social needs

36

Section Three

Kernels of Purpose

Kernels of Purpose

I am learning when we say, 'No' to the Lord, He often interprets that as a 'Yes.'

There's a generation that lives for their God given dream, but they have missed out on the everyday life that produces it.

I once said to the Lord, "I didn't get a thing out of that worship service." He said, "It's because I got it all."

"Don't try to glue your past together anymore. I'm pouring 'Miracle Grow' on your future."

Be careful, what has blessed you in the past could become a ball and chain around your feet to keep you from moving forward. (a stumbling block to make me falter + fall)

Be patient in transition, you are receiving a new transmission with upgraded gears. + hold me back

To all those who have ministered and have felt it didn't go well… I have been there. Sometimes you won't hit a home run. Sometimes just a base hit can bring someone home. what seems underwhelming

I always knew healing is found in the body of Christ, but now I know it's found in the joints of the body with whom He connects us with.

"Before you throw
the towel in,
wash someone's feet
with it and
you will find
yourself picking
it up again."

Section Four

Land Mines in the Fields

"Our delays

can be

God's

protection."

The Season to Ride Bulls

I sense this season will be like a rodeo bull ride for many of us. The stirrings, shakings and heavenly interruptions will feel like we are on a championship bull that defies us to hold onto it. We will need to learn quickly how to hold on and how to let go. This bull ride will expose what is in us. We must be fully persuaded that greater is He who is in us, than he who is in the world. And that He, Christ in us, is not afraid of being bullied by any bull.

Often After a Great Victory or Success Come the Greatest Defeats

After trusting the Lord with all your heart through blood, sweat and tears, with "eight" seconds of victory on a rodeo bull, when you fail to let go and exit quickly out of the electrifying arena, the bull begins to become the champion. It begins to attack the rider and retaliates with full blown death in his horns and hoofs that has been building up during those eight seconds. The standing and cheering ovation of the crowd changes to gasping and dread for the very life of the rider.

Spiritually, the number "eight" means "new beginnings." Many times at the height of success, in certain areas of our life and ministry, a new beginning has already started. This will allow you to enter into another area of your life, which will yield yet greater fruitfulness. "Nine" means "fruitfulness," so you better be off the bull by the end of eight seconds to catch up with your new beginning.

How to Exit the Arena That Made You a Champion

I have never seen one champion bull rider leave the arena without his face in the dirt, a limp, a wound, or a bruise of some sort. With all of the fame, every bone in his body is crying out with pain, and often there is help needed from others to help him get up and away from the bull that he had just overcome.

When you see someone being used greatly in ministry, and you think they are a champion in the Spirit, you don't know the pain that came with overcoming the enemy of their ministry. You will be able to tell the real champions from the false. They will walk with a limp, and if you look real close, they will have a tear running down their championship face. And perhaps to your surprise, they are not really confident after all, as their security has just been shaken to the very core of their being at the height of their success.

Many times, champions have difficulty limping off the field as they discover fresh revelation that God is calling them away from the bull or arena of ministry they had victory in.

43

I sense myself, as well as others, feel an accomplishment in some areas in ministry, and have seemingly experienced success as we have loved what we have been doing--especially when it seems to be blessing many others. But somehow I see many fingers besides mine, getting stuck around the rope of success, and God is announcing from the judges booth, high above the arena of champions to, "Let go now! I want you off the bull."

Perhaps the bull is your "Isaac" ministry that everyone has fallen in love with and your identity has become wrapped up in. I wonder if Abraham's fingers got stuck longer than eight seconds on the rope that he wrapped around his son Isaac when he was about to sacrifice him.

Let go of the rope of your success--to embrace your new beginnings, that may take you from being a championship bull rider, to a possible unknown, where the only person who may know you is God, so you will get to know Him all over again. Or who knows, maybe you will get to ride a bigger bull!

Come Unto Me All Ye "Champions" that Labor and Are Heavy Laden

I sense the Lord calling many of us, who have experienced some degree of success and even some degree of honor in ministry. Getting off of the bull can be risky and dangerous, but God is now reaching out His arms to catch us as we let go, and as we are seemingly thrown to the ground. He will bind our wounds, and pour in the oil and the wine to restore our souls.

Maybe I am alone in what I am experiencing in ministry. But in case there are perhaps thousands more out there, I want you to know you are not alone--God is with us. His new beginnings have already started for you and me.

It's in the letting go of the rope or ministry that we seal our spiritual championship. And that's "No Bull!"

"Brothers and sisters, I do not consider myself yet to have taken hold of it. But one thing I do: Forgetting what is behind and straining toward what is ahead, I press on toward the goal to win the prize for which God has called me heavenward in Christ Jesus."
Philippians 3:13-14 (NIV)

Sometimes We Need What We Don't Like

I was driving in a snowstorm when a huge truck ahead of me was going slower than I wanted. Although the roads were treacherous, I decided to take a risk and pass this humongous hindrance to make up for lost time. As I began to turn into the passing lane, I noticed a huge snow plow in front of the truck and it dawned on me that I needed to be behind the plow or I might never get to where I was going. Again, what I didn't like, I needed. Sometimes, our delays can be God's protection.

 "Be always humble, gentle, and patient. Show your love by being tolerant with one another." Ephesians 4:2 (GNT) Good News Translation

"Can These Bridges Hold the Weight of My Glory?"

Angels are descending to inspect spiritual bridges throughout the Body of Christ. As angels were inspecting 'Spiritual' bridges throughout the body of Christ, the Father was asking a question... "Can these bridges hold the weight of My glory?"

Webster's Dictionary defines the word "bridge" as: a structure spanning and providing passage over an "obstacle" as in a waterway.

Have you been feeling like there are obstacles in your road preventing you from getting to where God wants you to be?

Broken Roads...Broken Bridges

I sense many are now traveling down a broken road because of a broken bridge in their lives.

In times of war, if the enemy wants to paralyze a nation, he will target the bridges that connect the people in that nation to one another. Once disconnected, they have little power to resist the onslaught of their enemy.

I saw Many "Relationships" Representing "Bridges" throughout the Body of Christ Deteriorating and on the Verge of Collapsing

I saw some relationships representing bridges that were connecting the Body of Christ together, but had failed to be maintained over the years and now were on the verge of collapsing. The collapsing of these bridges would mean that many of us would be unable to cross over into our Kingdom purpose and destiny without these certain relationships being renewed, restored and strengthened.

Some relationships we once thought we could go on without, were now appearing before us as our *only* bridge to cross over into our inheritance. As I saw this, I sensed within me a proverb in the land stating, "I am not going anywhere without you and you are not going anywhere without me." Whether we liked each other or not, our opposing attitudes began to fade as we saw by revelation, "these bridges must be restored and updated!"

Many Dreams, Visions, Ministries and Even the Glory of God Will Experience Delays While this 'Bridge' Inspection is Going On!

The cries of those who were injured and wounded relationally through "spiritual" bridges that had collapsed were now being magnified and heard in the portals of Heaven! Angels were now being assigned as "bridge inspectors" to carefully inspect the infrastructure of those bridges to see if they were strong enough to carry the weight of the multitudes who would cross over into glory.

Many of God's people were seemingly going through the motions of forgiving one another, but were failing to be reconciled to each other. Many were loving each other from afar, yet still felt uncomfortable being close together to support the bridge God had called them to help build and to be a significant part of.

Don't Burn Any Bridges Behind You

I sensed the Lord saying to all of us, "Don't burn any bridges behind you." Let's not write off anyone in our lives we don't think we need anymore. About ten years ago, I was offended by a brother in another ministry that I thought I didn't need in my life. I was ready and justified to separate myself from this brother and his ministry. As I was about to sever my relationship with him, the Lord spoke to me, "You will need this brother and his ministry five years down the road from now to fulfill your destiny!"

Miracle Bridges are in the Making

Some who have tried to be reconciled with their loved ones and even their enemies, will discover that God has been faithfully working behind the scenes. He will honor those who have loved the unlovable and these faithful ones will begin seeing miracles take place to restore their collapsed bridge (which seemed impossible to rebuild). God will release miracles in many who have been faithful to hope against hope in their relationships to discover afresh that God's love can build a bridge!

Some Bridges Are Made to be Walked On

Have you ever felt like people were taking advantage

of you at times and seemingly walking on top of you? Welcome to the Kingdom of God! Besides having cars and trucks passing over them, some bridges are made to walk on. I know of one huge long bridge that is actually closed one day a year and the people are thrilled to walk across that great bridge.

With Three Nails and Two Pieces of Wood, Jesus Built a Bridge for You and Me

I sense the Cross is coming back into the construction site of many of our deteriorated and collapsed bridges. Death to self will be a powerful strengthening force to uphold these bridges. We must humble ourselves to prefer others and esteem their ministries and dreams even above our own. Crosses and nails will become a common ingredient to build these bridges that will eventually hold the weight of the Glory of God!

Welcome Bridge Builders....and don't forget those three nails and two pieces of wood.
"With all lowliness and meekness, with longsuffering, forbearing one another in love;" Ephesians 4:2 (KJV)

"*Marriages*

&

miracles

go together."

Do You Need a Miracle in Your Marriage?

Marriages are being bombarded by severe, raging storms like never before. Did you know that when you were even thinking about marriage, God was already thinking of miracles? God spells the word marriage... m-i-r-a-c-l-e. The Lord actually created marriages with a built-in need for miracles. The Lord ordained marriages to not only require miracles, but to demand them. Marriages demand miracles!

Marriages and Miracles Go Together

From Heaven's perspective, here is how it works. The Lord will allow the wine in your marriage to run out to get you on miracle territory... just like at the first marriage wedding feast in Cana! Did you know that when the Lord brought you and your spouse together, He knew you would need a miracle? In fact, there is something wrong if your marriage doesn't need a miracle sooner or later. Marriages and miracles just go together!

I believe Jesus chose to create His first miracle on earth where He knew it would be needed the most - at a wedding feast, so everyone will know they can have a miracle in their marriage. Study the couples throughout the Bible who had great destinies and you will find that they faced the greatest impossibilities and nothing less than a miracle brought them through to God's purposes.

Abraham and Sarah were destined to conceive and bring forth a son of promise. But "Houston, we have a problem!" Sarah wasn't able to conceive. Let's forget about this miracle stuff and get Hagar ("another woman is what I need") to fulfill my destiny..." so they thought.

A Man-Made Solution

Sarah agreed, "No, I don't have what it takes, go ahead and have Hagar... I am tired of this unfulfilled marriage" (paraphrased). Through painful experiences Abraham and Sarah learned that they needed more than each other (and a third party) to have their fulfillment in life. Finally, they realized that their answer was not in each other.

God waited until they both could not possibly have a child in the natural. Not only was Sarah's womb dead, but Abraham was about a hundred years old... out of commission also. They finally had to take their eyes off of themselves and look to the Lord realizing it was an "impossible mission." God was waiting all those years to hear from them what He knew all along... "WE NEED A MIRACLE IN OUR MARRIAGE!"

The Greater the Call on a Marriage - the Greater

the Need for Miracles!

In the first chapter of Luke, Zechariah and Elizabeth have an "impossible" area in their marriage. There is a barren place in their marriage also. Elizabeth could not conceive. Zechariah, a priest, was in the temple and had the greatest experience of his life. The Angel gave him the word of the Lord about his destiny of having John the Baptist for a son... representing the prophetic move coming to prepare the way of the Lord.

Luke 1:23 (KJV) *"...as soon as the days of his ministration (duties) in the temple were accomplished, he departed to HIS OWN HOUSE."* Then his wife Elizabeth who had been barren conceived! Many men today in the temple or ministry are being called by God to return to their own house to their own "barren" situations. Not until we men learn and experience spiritual intimacy with our own wife, so they can spiritually conceive, can we fulfill God's purpose for both of us in our marriage... and this includes bringing forth godly seed as well... children of destiny!

Wise Men Sought Jesus, but Mary Conceived Him!

Women are 'Conceivers' both physically and spiritually. Men are "Seekers." Ministries can go no further than marriages if we want children of destiny (godly seed). It's really out of spiritual intimacy with our spouse that ministry is birthed. I sense husbands and wives will have to hold hands (spiritually) to bring forth the next move of the Spirit. Men will have to cleave to their wives because it will take two for what God wants to do next. God is coming to couples in their own house in this hour.

Many men and women have received great visions and words from the Lord in churches. But the real conception of these words must take place in our home where we live. "Spiritual Conception" must also take place in our homes if we are going to see our destiny fulfilled and the Kingdom of God advance. Have we men failed to take home what we receive in God's House and neglect spiritual intimacy with our wives at home?

I sense the wine (intimacy) has run out in many marriages, but I hear the Lord saying to the angels, "Get the water pots and fill them with water. I'm going to turn water into wine again and marriages into miracles. I have saved My best wine that has been aging for centuries for this last hour. I have saved the best wine for last to be tasted right at home between husband and wife."

Is there spiritual barrenness in your marriage? Need a great miracle? Your great need for a miracle qualifies you to receive one! They say marriages are made in Heaven... so is lightning and thunder. Expect miracles in your marriage today!

"Husbands, love your wives, just as Christ loved the church and gave himself up for her." Ephesians 5:25 (NIV)

Why Many Prophetic Words Don't Come to Pass

When we receive a true prophetic word from the Lord I believe it will be awhile before we are ready for another one. There will be homework to do and some tests to take. *"Until the word of the Lord came to Joseph, the word of the Lord tried him."* Psalm 105:19. With Joseph's prophetic dream came a lot of homework. His first assignment was to learn how to handle being betrayed and thrown into a pit.

His mid-term test was to see how fast he could run from Potiphar's wife. After being falsely accused, his final exam was taken in prison. It took him many long years to finish it. One final question for extra credit was: How do you handle being overlooked when you help someone else get promoted to freedom? After living out the right answer for two more years in prison, he received his diploma and graduated to the palace!

We must remember what God's dream is for us. He is dreaming about us being changed into the image and likeness of his Son, Jesus. Then everything else falls into place.

"For those God foreknew he also predestined to be conformed to the image of his Son, that he might be the firstborn among many brothers and sisters."

Romans 8:29 (NIV)

"Don't count

your money,

read it!"

These Words Are Putting Locks and Chains on Wallets and Churches

In the Spirit, I saw words coming out of the mouths of God's people that appeared to be forming chain-like links hooking together. With each negative comment, our words became like a chain that grew, wrapping itself around the object we were complaining about.

One of the largest chains I saw was wrapping around finances. Each time someone would say, "I don't have enough money," this chain became reinforced with strength, wrapping more tightly around their wallets and purses. As this complaining continued, I saw huge locks come upon these chains as a spirit of poverty and depression begin to fulfill the words that were being spoken.

I saw enormous chains come over whole ministries and churches.

Wherever two or more people were gathered together and began to say, "We don't have enough money for this or that in our ministry or church," huge chains began to wrap around whole ministries, congregations, pulpits and altar rails.

I saw a muzzle come over the mouths of many pastors when just a few members were agreeing and saying, "We can't afford to pay him that much!"

Chains started growing around the pastor's whole family as the spirit of poverty continued to increase in churches, like a little leaven leavening the whole lump. I saw churches closing as chains and locks were being installed on their front doors. The spirit of poverty overcame many, stopping them from giving tithes and offerings.

I then saw in the Spirit one person stand up in a church that was about to close its doors. This person lifted his wallet towards heaven and thanked God that he even had a wallet. Though nothing was inside it, he was praising God that he had the breath to praise Him in spite of his lack of finances. As this man started lifting up his wallet with thanksgiving and praise, the chain snapped off it, and the Lord spoke audibly to this church, *"Let everything that has breath, praise Me! In everything give thanks, for this is the will of God in Christ Jesus concerning you and this house."* 1 Thessalonians 5:18 (KJV)

A revelation was breaking forth upon God's people that just breathing qualifies us to praise and worship Him. "In God We Trust" became a sermon as someone pulled out their last dollar bill and began to read what was written on their money instead of counting how much they didn't have. God spoke. "Don't count your money—read it! Count on Me!"

Ministries, churches and their members were being freed as chains and locks began to melt from the presence of the Lord as they discovered God was their source.

A fresh oil of giving flowed upon God's people as they became thankful. As they started thanking God for their wallets and purses, though empty and needy, I saw a key being turned in the door of a bank in heaven filling wallets, purses, ministries and churches with whatever they needed.

I saw the future of many churches so blessed and prosperous from members giving freely that pastors had to announce to their congregations. "We have enough money! Please pray to see where God would have us use the extra finances that have come in."

It seemed when God's people began to give thanks, they discovered blessings and finances they didn't know they had. It would come from somewhere, somehow, because of their heart of thanksgiving in wanting to give instead of receive. They wanted to bless others, and in turn, money seemed to come looking for them and track them down, overtaking them with material and spiritual blessings that they couldn't put a price tag on.

Each time a ministry, church or individual would say, "We have enough money, for God is our source," angels would be released to bring in above and beyond what they were believing God for.

"May these words of my mouth and this meditation of my heart be pleasing in your sight, LORD, my Rock and my Redeemer." Psalm 19:14 (NIV)

Spiritual Water Competitions Are Now Forbidden

I believe the Lord is going to use us under water more. Surface competition never advances God's kingdom. He's building His kingdom in spiritual waters.

"Your steps formed a highway through the seas with footprints on a pathway no one even knew was there." Psalm 77:19 (TPT)

Don't Forget the Duct Tape

I read where duct tape is sent on every space mission from NASA. If it wasn't for duct tape Apollo 13 would not have survived getting back to earth. I believe when the Lord sends us on His mission, He is saying, "Don't forget the duct tape." Have you ever wished you wouldn't have said what you said to someone or even to yourself?" I have lost more than one battle by answering the enemy.

Sometimes the best thing is to ignore him. The next time you are tempted to say something to someone or yourself from your emotions, wait 24 hours, then rip the duct tape from your mouth and pray before you speak.

"Everyone should be quick to listen, slow to speak and slow to become angry." James 1:19 (NIV)

"If you keep talking, it won't be long before you're saying something really wrong. Prove you're wise from the very start— just bite your tongue and be strong!" Proverbs 10:19 (TPT)

A Missing Part of Prayer

I just experienced a missing part of prayer. It's been years since I tasted it. It's when you pray about something until there's a sweet release of its burden. Saints of old called it - 'praying through'. It's like I prayed myself out of myself and there's no need to pray any further because you have God's peace on it. You know that you know it's gonna be ok.

Let me ask you, "How long has it been since you knelt on your knees and prayed til your heart knew no burden? I think it's been too long for most of us.

"Elijah was a human being, even as we are. He prayed earnestly that it would not rain, and it did not rain on the land for three and a half years." James 5:17 (NIV)

"Doubt Your Doubts and Trust Me."

Have you ever second guessed yourself? You step out and do something you thought for sure was the Lord. Then this flood of doubt hits you and you second guess yourself.

It can be tormenting. This morning the Lord nailed it for me, "When I thought you up before you were conceived in your mother's womb, 'I Never Second Guessed You. I Had No Doubts About You!'

"So don't second guess yourself by doubting Me. I'll

let you know if you get off track. Doubt your doubts and trust Me."

"But when you ask, you must believe and not doubt, because the one who doubts is like a wave of the sea, blown and tossed by the wind." James 1:6 (NIV)

Is the Lord Still Sharpening You?

Those who hang out with friends who seem to see eye-to-eye on everything and never disagree, will not grow much. I sense the enemy has been working overtime trying to convince many that you no longer need the irritation and grinding of certain people in your life. Be careful! The Lord may still be sharpening you. The person who is least like you and sees things so differently, may be the best asset for your future purpose in God's Kingdom.

"As iron sharpens iron, so one person sharpens another." Proverbs 27:17 (NIV)

"Do you love religious people?"

Do You Have a Religious Spirit?

The Lord spoke to me personally. "Son, you have been faithful in hating religious spirits, but you have fallen short in loving religious people. I love them. I want to deliver them. Not loving them invites a religious spirit into your life."

"For in the same way you judge others, you will be judged, and with the measure you use, it will be measured to you." Matthew 7:2 (NIV)

The Power of Life and Death Is in Our Tongue

If a coin was found in a fish's mouth, maybe there is a connection between our mouth and our money. How many times have we said, "I'm broke, I'm sick, I'm catching a cold," and watched it come to pass? Little do we realize that when we open our mouth we are prophesying either good or bad! Why not say, "I have all the money I will ever need! I'm being attacked by healing! Healing runs in my family! I heard a saying once that even a fish would stay out of trouble if it learned to keep its mouth shut!

"The tongue has the power of life and death, and those who love it will eat its fruit." Proverbs 18:21 (NIV)

"Hell

trembles

because you

are still

alive."

When the Devil Says, "You Missed It!" You Probably Hit the Bulls Eye!

The devil never wants you to know how much God is using you. He is using you more than you know. Hell trembles because you are still alive. The devil's greatest fear is: You are still here. He has heard how God has rescued you and changed your life.

He heard about the fiery furnace you were in and he saw the fourth man show up. He saw your Red Sea split open. He saw the Lion's Den you were in and saw the mouths of the Lions shut. He has heard about your God who is now causing you to take your family, city and nation! When the devil says, "You missed it," you probably hit the bull's eye!

"He was a murderer from the beginning, not holding to the truth, for there is no truth in him. When he lies, he speaks his native language, for he is a liar and the father of lies." John 8:4 (NIV)

When Mothers Pray, Hell Trembles

The most dangerous person on earth is a praying mother. My mother had such a prayer life, that when us kids would come home late at night, she would tell us where we were and what we were doing. It took the fun out of sinning early in life.

And she would do awful things like make us go to church when we didn't want to.

Thanks Mom.

"Honor your father and your mother, so that you may live long in the land the LORD your God is giving you." Exodus 20:12 (NIV)

Doing the PRACTICAL to Release the SUPERNATURAL

"But Jehoshaphat said, 'Is there not here a prophet of the LORD, that we may inquire of the LORD by him?' And one of the king of Israel's servants answered and said, 'Here is Elisha the son of Shaphat, who poured water on the hands of Elijah.' And Jehoshaphat said, 'The word of the LORD is with him.' So the king of Israel and Jehoshaphat and the king of Edom went down to him." 2 Kings 3:11-12 (KJV)

It is believed that Elisha spent his first ten years

ministering to Elijah. Even after Elijah departed, he was known as "Elisha...who used to pour water on the hands of Elijah." Elijah was known as a lonely prophet and ended up battling depression in a cave thinking he was the only one left that was living for God at that time.

Elisha's ministry doubled in miracles, seemingly with less fanfare with the emphasis more on serving compassion to people. Elisha seemed to even downplay the "hoop de lah" of miracles and seemed to weave the practical side of life into the miraculous, showing that in our everyday, ordinary activities lies the "stuff" that leads us into the supernatural realm of miracles, signs and wonders!

The Supernatural at Work in our Everyday Ordinary Lives

The word practical means "pertaining to be useful in ordinary everyday activities or work."

In 2 Kings 5:1-14 (KJV), you can read the whole story of how Naaman, captain of the host of the king of Syria, a great man with his master and very honorable, received his miracle in a very practical, ordinary way. It starts with a little maid who was taken captive out of the land of Israel who waited on Naaman's wife. She said to Naaman's wife (verse 3), *"Would God my lord were with the prophet that is in Samaria! for he would recover him of his leprosy."*

This great miracle begins with a little maid wanting to do good to Naaman, although she had been taken captive by his soldiers. It must have been humbling to Naaman to listen to this little, captive maid and start his journey for his healing to see this prophet, Elisha. 2 Kings 5:9, (KJV) *"So Naaman came...and stood at the door of the house of Elisha."*

Elisha sends a messenger to him saying (verse 10): *"Go and wash in Jordan seven times, and thy flesh shall come again to thee, and thou shalt be clean."* Naaman gets upset for he doesn't even get to see the prophet make a big deal of his healing (verse 11): *"I thought, He will surely come out to me, and stand, and call on the name of the LORD his God, and strike his hand over the place, and recover the leper."*

Naaman even thought that this prophet picked the wrong river to go dipping in. He knew of better rivers that he preferred, and anger rose up in Naaman (verse 13): *"And his servants came near and spake unto (Naaman), and said, 'My father, if the prophet had bid thee to do some great thing, wouldest thou not have done it? How much rather then, when he saith to thee, 'Wash, and be clean?'"* Naaman finally obeyed and was healed of his leprosy.

Can you see the practical things the prophet told Naaman to do to receive his healing? Naaman never even got to see the prophet Elisha until after his healing! I believe Elisha learned through serving Elijah many years by doing many practical things, such as pouring water on Elijah's hands, that supernatural miracles and healings began right there.

Jesus Went About Doing Good to People; as a Result, Healings and Miracles Followed.

"How God anointed Jesus of Nazareth with the Holy Ghost and power: who went about doing good, and healing all that were oppressed of the devil; for God was with Him." Acts 10:38 (KJV)

Lately, as I've read this verse, the words "doing good" jumped out at me. Imagine Jesus being filled with the Holy Ghost and power and all He wants to do with all that power is to just walk around "doing good" to people! It sounds like healing and miracles were not the first thing on His mind. Of course, healings and miracles took place, but it was the result of His love and compassion to help people.

His passion was people, not healings or miracles. Whatever it took to do good to people would then take place, even if it took a miracle or healing, for He wanted to do good! Signs and wonders followed Him as His compassion moved Him towards people. It seems that "doing good" things, which included practical things like holding children in His arms, eating with publicans and sinners, and letting a prostitute wash his dirty feet, often released revelation that others needed to experience the supernatural.

Recently, I had a dream where someone was holding a crying child that could not be comforted. As the person handed me the child to hold, it became calm and peaceful in my arms. As I was holding this child, I saw a small gift wrapped at my feet that began to leak out like a small drop of oil from the inside of it. At first, I thought some kind of bottle with liquid inside the gift must have broken and caused this drop to appear on the ground.

As I continued to hold the child, this dripping continued out of this gift until it began to flow freely all over the floor without stopping. People were being drawn to what appeared to be oil flowing from this gift that was still wrapped up. I knew that by my just holding and comforting this troubled child, it was causing this awesome anointing oil to be released from this small gift.

God was showing me something. "Bill, if you are willing to begin to take your eyes off of your so-called gifting and are willing to do some practical, needed things in people's lives, My anointing will begin to flow out of your life as a result of you getting closer to people, instead of you focusing on your gift." I, for one, plan to be more sensitive to small children.

Did the Five Thousand Know Their 'Miracle' Meal was Catered by a Little Boy's Lunch?

In Luke 9:13 (KJV), Jesus said to His disciples when they wanted to send the multitudes away, "You give them something to eat!" And then He told His disciples to make the multitude sit down by fifties in a company.

Imagine the practicality of having the disciples getting five thousand men, besides the women and children, to sit down by fifties! And then as Jesus blessed the five loaves and two fishes, He gave them to His disciples to hand out...now that's "practical hospitality."

Notice the practical things the disciples did which were woven into this miracle. This all seems so practical, but watch what happens...here comes a miracle on the heels of "practicality"!

I don't read anywhere that a big announcement was made to the multitude that their meal was catered by a little boy's bag lunch. Jesus didn't seem to make a big deal out of the miracle. He even made it look like the disciples fed them all! This miracle looked so practical in the making.

Of course, the miracle of multiplying the food took place, but His priority was to get those five thousand growling stomachs so full that there would be twelve baskets left over! Since it took a miracle to feed these people, that's what Jesus used. The miracle was just part of the journey of His goal to feed them.

This miracle seemed to have practical applications woven all throughout it, beginning with the mother who fixed an ordinary bag lunch for her son. Was Jesus teaching His disciples that in doing the practical, every day, ordinary, mundane things of doing good for people lies the ingredients of the supernatural?

As I Watched My New Neighbor's Grass Grow Taller, The Lord Spoke Clearly to Me, "Mow it Without Telling Her I Told You To."

"They shall fear (the Lord) as long as the sun and moon endure (as long as the light is shining), throughout all generations. He shall come down like rain upon the mown grass: as showers that water the earth!" Psalm 72:5-6 (KJV)

I started to mow my neighbor's yard several times and no one seemed to notice it. I found out later the neighbor woman had no husband or lawn mower. She was too busy to even thank me at first, for she was never home with having to work two jobs. She finally did thank me and said she couldn't afford to pay me, but I knew that as I mowed her lawn that something was happening in the Spirit. Every place where the souls of my feet were coming down, God was giving me favor and influence; in this case it was by just mowing the lawn. And as verse 7 says, "He shall come down like rain upon the mown grass."

With each rain that fell upon this neighbor's mown grass, God was coming down upon this family! At first, I wanted to tell her that God had spoken to me to mow her grass for the summer, but the Lord seemed to stop me and wanted me to just let His light shine through me without getting Him involved prematurely. I am sure, like others, she has met Christians who have disappointed her because of their lack of follow-through or un-Christ-like actions.

Now is the time to do something good to help others see the light at the end of the tunnel. I believe it's time for us to show people we personally care about them, before we even begin to mention how much God cares.

I believe the Lord is highlighting the need to be practical in our approach to this lost and dying world. It's past time to put shoe leather on our prayers and worship, and overcome evil with good.

When Life is Over We Will Be Judged by the 'Practical' Things We Were All Capable of Doing, But Didn't

"When the Son of man shall come in His glory, and

all the holy angels with Him, then shall He sit upon the throne of His glory: And before Him shall be gathered all nations: and He shall separate them one from another, as a shepherd divideth his sheep from the goats..." Matthew 25:31-46 (KJV)

"Then shall the King say unto them on His right hand, 'Come, ye blessed of My Father, inherit the kingdom prepared for you from the foundation of the world: For I was hungry, and ye gave Me meat: I was thirsty, and ye gave Me drink: I was a stranger, and ye took Me in: Naked, and ye clothed Me: I was sick, and ye visited Me: I was in prison, and ye came unto Me."

As we are moved with compassion to minister to people's practical needs, I believe we will experience more of the power of God upon us, so we can be used to release the supernatural into their lives as well.

Romans 2:4 (NKJV) says, *"...the goodness of God leads you to repentance."* Let's go about doing good and watch the supernatural take place.

Section Five

Your Life Has Purpose

"Our

boot camp

is over."

Don't Go AWOL! The Enemy is Trembling Because of You

I heard hell screaming: "Where did they come from?"

The Lord of hosts was shouting: "They are My sneak surprise!"

The enemy will soon know why you haven't been heard from. He thought you gave up. He didn't realize that your long season of hiddenness, hardships, and lonely, dark nights were blessings in disguise, for they had come to train you. Even your enemies were being used to equip you. The devil thought we quit, but he is in for a big surprise. Our boot camp is over!

"Endure suffering along with me, as a good soldier of Christ Jesus. Soldiers don't get tied up in the affairs of civilian life, for then they cannot please the officer who enlisted them." 2 Timothy 2:3,4 (NLT)

Unlearned and Ignorant Men Turned the World Upside Down

Unlearned and ignorant men turned the world upside down. Their only credentials were: They had been with Jesus.

"Now when they saw the boldness of Peter and John, and perceived that they were unlearned and ignorant men, they marveled; and they took knowledge of them, that they had been with Jesus." Acts 4:13 (KJV)

Maybe we need to unlearn some things. Maybe we ought to come to God stupid every day and just be with Him.

Oh, this is such good preaching!

"Second fiddle

is actually

a promotion."

I'm Calling Many to Play Second Fiddle

A famous conductor once shared that the most difficult instrument to play is the second fiddle.

'Would You Be Willing to Play Second Fiddle for Me?'

I sense a special invitation is going out to many in this hour who have been faithful in certain key positions and have blessed others with their giftings and callings. I see these individuals as anointed ones who have been blessed to play "first" place violin or fiddle in God's orchestra. Let me add that when you are in first place being used as an instrument, there are times when all eyes and ears are upon you, especially when you are ministering a solo part in God's kingdom. The pressure is on you as the enemy is working overtime against you to miss a note.

As this picture unfolded, I saw heaven's spotlight dimming off of many first-place positions and calling many of us to greater promotions in the kingdom by humbling ourselves under someone else to help raise them up above and beyond ourselves.

Freedom and a Creative Anointing Is Rising Upon "Second" Fiddlers

It's interesting to learn that second fiddlers actually

have a greater freedom and creativity to play more notes than the solo fiddler. They are released to harmonize and do whatever they desire to make the first-place fiddler sound his very best. Though he is in the background, he often, through his creativity is the one who covers many mistakes of the one in the spotlight.

Joseph was exalted to the palace to play second fiddle to Pharaoh and to all of Joseph's family. All of Egypt heard the sound of heavenly harmony. Genesis 41:40,43 and 50:18-22 (KJV)

Pharaoh says to Joseph, *"You will be over my house, and according to your word all my people will be ruled."* Gen. 41:40 (KJV) And in verse 43, *"Then he [Pharaoh] had him [Joseph] ride in the second chariot which was his."* Gen. 41:43a. (KJV)

Then his brothers also went and fell down before his face and said, *"We are your servants."* Joseph said to them, *"Do not be afraid, for am I in the place of God? But as for you, you intended to harm me, but God intended it for good, in order to bring it about as it is this day, to save many lives. So now, do not fear. I will provide for you and your little ones."* So he comforted them and spoke kindly to them. Joseph stayed in Egypt, he and his father's household, and Joseph lived one hundred and ten years."* Genesis 50:18-22 (KJV)

Second Fiddle Is Actually Promotion

"This I know: the favor that brings promotion and power doesn't come from anywhere on earth, for no one exalts a person but God, the true judge of all. He alone determines where favor rests. He anoints one for greatness and brings another down to his knees."
Psalm 75:6-8 (TPT)

I used to think that when God puts down one, it is a demotion, but not from God's perspective. It is all part of God's process to promote us to greater purposes. Ask Joseph how he arrived at the palace, and he will make sure you understand what the pit and the prison did to get him there, and how fast he ran to flee from Potiphar's wife. Joseph had integrity that kept him when his God-given dream was coming to pass. His gifts and dreams brought him to the palace, but his integrity kept him there.

When God brings us low, it's in order to raise us up higher, not in our eyes, but in His. God has many members in His body, and He won't use us all the time. If He did, we would burn out. If you are in a low place right now, be encouraged, for you are on your way up. If you are being greatly used, don't be surprised if the Lord chooses to bring you to a place of greater humility to refine your gift and character.

Anyone ready to play second fiddle? May Jesus have first place in all we do, and may we follow His example of lifting up others to give Him all the glory.

"Let nothing be done through strife or vainglory; but in lowliness of mind let each esteem other better than themselves. 4 Look not every man on his own things, but every man also on the things of others." Phil. 2:3-4. (KJV)

I'm Giving My People a Million Dollar Voice

I heard the Lord say, "I'm giving My people a 'million-dollar' voice this year. It won't be just saying the right words but how they say it. Speaking from a right spirit will produce million-dollar results.

"When they speak, it will be worth a million dollars to the listener, for I am giving their voice a certain sound that when they speak, even the birds will hush their singing. Their spoken-right words will resound in the bones and marrow of people.

"Their words will save, heal, deliver and people will say, 'What you said was worth a million dollars to me,' for My people will speak by My Spirit, not by their flesh."

"A word fitly spoken is like apples of gold in pictures of silver." Prov. 25:11 (KJV)

What Part of the Word 'GO' Do You Not Understand?

I sense the Father saying, "I am hungry for My harvest!"

Upon hearing these words, and realizing we are the Lord's body on earth, could it be that the insatiable hunger that God has put into many of us may not be just for Him alone, but could it also be for His harvest?

Sustenance in the Harvest Fields

When I think in the natural, I know that at harvest times it's important to bring in the harvest because it is our food and sustenance. The natural harvest sustains our life and health. Could it be that, as in the natural harvest, the spiritual harvest holds far more for us than we realize? Could the spiritual harvest also hold spiritual nourishment that we have lacked in our walk, even with God? Could there be sustenance in the harvest fields that we have yet to discover, that haven't been found in our churches and gatherings? I personally believe there is.

When Jesus was ministering to the woman at the well, and the disciples returned with food, they wondered why He was no longer hungry. In John 4:32, Jesus says, *"I have food to eat of which you do not know."*

The disciples thought someone had actually brought Jesus something to eat. He then explains in verse 34, *"My food is to do the will of Him who sent Me, and to finish His work."* And in verse 35, Jesus tells His disciples to *"lift up your eyes and look at the fields, for they are already white for harvest."*

I believe Jesus was showing us through His own experience that it is in reaching out to the lost that we get true nourishment and satisfaction in our own lives. Sounds like Jesus got something in the harvest field that He didn't get in the temple. I believe the Lord has put such a high priority on reaching the lost that there are also wages and rewards given that we haven't experienced until we actually go. The devil will tell you, "Don't go until you feel good enough and prepared." But it's in the "going" that God equips us and anoints us in the harvest fields. You will discover that the harvest anointing is in the harvest itself. The harvest anointing will take care of a whole lot of your problems.

'There Are Harvest Healings and Harvest Miracles Waiting for Us'

My mother, who has been healed so many times and lived to be 90 years old, found the key to long life. I once heard her pray when the doctor discovered a tumor on her thyroid. Before the biopsy test, she prayed to the Lord, "Father, if I get sick and weak with this tumor, how will I be able to serve You and reach the lost?"

All I know is that the next morning when the doctor went to take a biopsy, they couldn't find that tumor. I believe many times the Lord wants to know why we want to be healed; not so we can live a long life ... but why do we want to live a long life? Is it for Him and others, or just for ourselves?

I believe the harvest this hour is so ripe that as we reach out and walk into these harvest fields, many of us will discover not only the lost being touched, but we ourselves will find nourishment so sustaining that healings and deliverances will be taking place in our own lives. There are harvest healings and harvest miracles waiting for us.

Do you have a great hunger for God that refuses to be satisfied? Follow Jesus into the harvest fields. You will find meat to eat that's only found through reaching out to the lost. And why are you still waiting when Jesus already said, "Go!"

"What part of the word 'go!' do you not understand?"

"Now go in my authority and make disciples of all nations, baptizing them in the name of the Father, the Son, and the Holy Spirit. And teach them to faithfully follow[a] all that I have commanded you. And never forget that I am with you every day, even to the completion of this age." Matthew 28:19 -20b (TPT)

"Extreme

trials and

extreme

victories..."

We Slay Bears, We Slay Lions and We Slay Giants

I sense we are entering a season of 'everything at once'. All hell will break loose and all of heaven will break loose, but heaven is greater than hell. I sense the presence of a great cloud of heavenly witnesses, including family members, standing to cheer us on in this coming year. The eyes of heaven are upon us, waving checkered flags in the distance.

The heavens are shouting, "Don't lose your excitement for what God has called you to do. Your excitement excites Him and activates the angels among you. Excitement is a powerful weapon against the enemy, as it ties his hands."

A challenging year is ahead. It will seem like everything is happening at the same time. People will be saying, "*It's always something. It's always something,*" in a negative tone. On the other hand, if we stay focused on the Lord, we will be saying, "*He's always doing something. He's always doing something good, in spite of the situation.*"

The mindset we need to have at this time is: "We slay bears, we slay lions and we slay giants. That's what we do, that's who we are." For they will come this year to find out what is in us. These will be distractions to keep us from focusing on the Lord and worshipping Him no matter what. I sense the enemy saying, "I hope you don't feel like worshipping the Lord this year with what I have in mind. If you do, it will bring Him down into your situation, and if He shows up, I'm out of here, for He doesn't know how to lose. Defeat is not in Him."

Extreme Trials and Extreme Victories

It will be a season like Houston being hit by a hurricane and winning the World Series in the same year; extreme testings and extreme victories. Testings will bring them on. Priorities will change as these challenges show up.

I hear the Father saying, "Batten Down the Hatches." I sense this means the prayer closet will become a very important place in our lives. "Batten down the hatches," I sense, refers to closing the door on distractions as we not only pray, but listen to Him speaking to us.

I See Bear Rugs, Lion Furs and Giants' Heads on Gold Platters

This will be a time when mighty men and mighty women will rise up because they've killed a bear, a lion or a giant, for these have come to make us strong. God says, "They will be your nourishment, your bread, your sustenance." We will get to eat honey out of the belly of the lion. We will see what a lion's fur looks like hanging in our house, and we will see the heads of giants on gold platters. I see bear rugs, lion furs and giants' heads laid all over the place in your house. These will be trophies awarded to those who didn't give up the good fight of faith.

Giants Are the Breakfast of Champions

I hear the Father asking, "How hungry are you? When you get hungry enough, you get to eat giants! The giants aren't showing up to take you out, they're showing up so you can eat them. Eat your giants today. They are your nourishment. They are your bread and sustenance. Giants are the breakfast of champions."

"Only do not rebel against the Lord, nor fear the people of the land because they are bread for us. Their defense is gone from them, and the Lord is with us. Do not fear them" (Num. 14:9) (KJV)

I have wondered why it's still my favorite song. "I'm no longer a slave to fear; I am a child of God." Why is "Do Not Fear" mentioned so often throughout the Bible? It's because God knows there will be times and reasons when we will be afraid, but He is with us. He has already slain every bear, every lion and every giant we will ever face, so we can too. Remember: Jesus lives in us, He is not afraid and He doesn't worry about anything.

"Have I not commanded you? Be strong and courageous. Do not be afraid; do not be discouraged, for the LORD your God will be with you wherever you go." Joshua 1:9 (NIV)

Spiritual Weather Forecast: A Writer's Storm Is Coming!

I just read the late breaking news on the winter storm approaching the East Coast, where I live. As I read the headlines, instead of the word "winter," I saw the word "writer." I then knew this was the Lord speaking to me. I heard Him say, "A writers' storm is coming! I'm sending a storm of writers who will write with the pen of transparency of heart and revelation. Their words will seem at first like innocent snowflakes falling. Then without warning, these words will gather momentum, causing spiritual blizzard conditions with avalanches of My Spirit falling on the hearts of nations."

My Roof-Tearing Angels Have Been Released

"Palaces and prisons will witness miracles appearing like snow falling inside of them as their roof tops weaken under the heavy snowfall of My glory coming from this writer's storm. No house is exempt. These writings under My unction will have built-in radar to find their readers. Men, women and children, weary and worn, will rise again to take the kingdoms of this world. My roof-tearing angels have been released and they have your address."

"This writer's storm will not end with Spring approaching. It will snowball throughout this summer and the rest of the year and continue storming the gates of hell until Jesus comes." I keep seeing angels with slingshots, hurling books into the new year, hitting the foreheads of giants. Keep writing!"

"Praise be to the LORD my Rock, who trains my hands for war, my fingers for battle." Psalm 144:1 (NIV)

"I want to release a 'hammer anointing.'"

If I Had a Hammer

Right before our New Jersey ministry trip our car wouldn't start. Triple A road service hit the starter with a hammer and it started right up. Being too late for a mechanic to put a new starter on our car, I asked a seasoned mechanic, "What should I do?" He said, "Take a hammer with you and if it doesn't start, hit the starter with a hammer!" I said, "Do you mean I am going to New Jersey by the way of a hammer?" The next morning, we left and never had to use the hammer. The car kept starting for us. God spoke to me on the way. "I want to release a 'hammer anointing' throughout the state of New Jersey."

I used the hammer in every meeting to hit some things that God wanted to start back up; things that had been stopped such as ministries, as well as to start some new things for His kingdom. His word, like a hammer, came down on injustice, generational curses, the political realm and so many other things. His hammer struck so hard that I heard the Liberty Bell ring in Philadelphia. The claw of the hammer was used to loosen things in the Spirit. God really does use the foolish things for His glory. Who knows how far God's hammer will travel across this nation and around the world. A precious brother there put a new starter on our car as a gift from the Lord before we left. Your prayers work wonders for us.

"Is not my word like fire," declares the LORD, "and like a hammer that breaks a rock in pieces?" Jeremiah 23a; 29 (NIV)

"Your Trusting Will Be Your Training."

I said to the Lord, "Why are you not making things clear to us? What will our next phase of life and ministry look like?" He answered, "Because I don't want you to mess it up." He did explain one thing. "There will be times that I will use you and many others in areas where you have had no specific training. Trust Me. Your trusting will be your training."

"Trust in the Lord with all your heart and lean not on your own understanding; in all your ways submit to him, and he will make your paths straight." Proverbs 3:5-6 (NIV)

Section Six

The One Who Owns the Cattle on a Thousand Hills is in Your Gleaning Fields

"I'm Ripping the Hinges Off of Closed Doors"

Man has overlooked you, but I am going to overbook you!

I just heard the Father saying, "Many who have been hidden and overlooked with doors slamming in their faces, I am going to overbook you with opportunities. You've been waiting in the wings, but I'm giving you wings. No more eagles in the chicken coop! You're going to fly!"

"For promotion cometh neither from the east, nor from the west, nor from the south. But God is the judge: he putteth down one, and setteth up another." Psalm 75:6-7 (KJV)

"Quit saying,

'I am

getting

older.'"

Prophetic Alert: "I Am Breaking the Age Barrier!"

I hear the Father saying, "I am breaking the age barrier! Quit saying, 'I am getting older.' Christ in you is ageless. Allow His Spirit to quicken your mortal body and soar with the Eagles. And don't tell Me where I can't send you this year. Get over yourself and buy some new luggage." (Someone should be shouting about now!)

"With long life will I satisfy him, and shew him my salvation." Psalm 91:16 (KJV)

God is Picking Up His Paint Brush

God is using chaos and gross darkness as His canvas and He is picking up His paint brush. The ashes of our dreams mixed with tears have become God's paint. It will be an oil painting, for He is stirring in the oil of joy. A brilliant portrait is coming forth to light up the world. Be still...it's you!

"To provide for them that mourn in Zion, to give unto them beauty for ashes, the oil of joy for mourning, the garment of praise for the spirit of heaviness; that

they might be called trees of righteousness, the planting of the LORD, that he might be glorified." Isaiah 61:3 (KJV)

"He was

the uninvited

guest who

invited

Himself."

It's Showtime!

In the spirit, I saw on giant marquees in front of theaters, hotels and many buildings throughout the world, the words, "It's Showtime!" The Lord was announcing to planet earth that He was coming to show up in a sovereign way to heal, deliver and manifest His glory.

It was a kairos time to show and tell cities and nations what He had to offer. Just when we thought every light on earth had gone out and the stars had fallen from their sockets, His light was returning to the world, expelling darkness.

I was amazed as I saw Him overruling people's belief systems and revealing Himself to them. He was touching atheists who didn't believe in Him, but He believed in them. Witches, occults, Hollywood stars and many of His own people, who through great trials, afflictions and hope deferred, had turned away from Him were still being pursued by Him.

It was a day of His appearing once again as He was making public appearances throughout the world by visions and dreams to individuals, including world leaders and mass gatherings. To many, He was the uninvited guest who had invited Himself.

"And it shall come to pass afterward, that I will pour out my spirit upon all flesh; and your sons and your

daughters shall prophesy, your old men shall dream dreams, your young men shall see visions." Joel 2:28 (KJV)

The Tide is Turning!

I saw the Spirit of the Lord as a great ocean beginning to recede off an enormous shore line. This was a season in time when "the tide" was beginning to go out. The Body of Christ was standing in the water, practically immersed in the tide. But as the tide gradually began to go out, we began to gradually be exposed as though we could no longer be covered by the water. It seemed we stood spiritually naked as the tide was still going out.

As the tide went out from the shoreline, many chains and bondages could be seen holding God's people. This was hindering them and stopping them from going on to follow the Spirit, which was gradually going out from them, leaving them helpless and powerless as though the Spirit was exposing their sin and weakness, yet at the same time, departing from them.

Others were able to go further on after His Spirit, but

the tide seemed to pick up a faster pace, and there was a great cry as the tide rapidly went out and even the very elect and righteous began to cry out, "My God, my God, why hast Thou forsaken me?" As the Body of Christ stood still with exhaustion and weariness and great discouragement, the ground beneath turned into dry land, where there was no water-- like a desert.

The Church could only see the tide going out a long way off and could no longer experience the move of the Spirit. On the contrary, what was left was their sins, bondages, and helplessness. As the Church was exposed and stood as though naked, a great mocking cry was heard from those who were back on the shore who had never touched the water. This represented the world, and they were seeing the shame and sin, and God was being reproached. The time frame this was happening in seemed like forever to God's people--as though they were separated from God and nothing appeared to be happening, except for failure.

Many turned from looking towards the tide going out, and after a while, they began to walk back towards the shore from where they came. They just gave up and were tired of waiting and waiting, convinced that God had forsaken them by all appearances.

But a remnant stayed and stood still, waiting upon

the Lord, confessing their sins and repenting and interceding for all the world, realizing it is not by might, nor by power, but only by the Spirit of the Living God. Then it seemed that the earth stood still, and the waters going out even stopped and a strange calmness came. And then the Lord spoke: "The tide is beginning to turn. The tide is beginning to turn. And the tide is on its way back in! This is the tsunami of My glory that My earth has been waiting for!"

It was wave after wave after wave. These waves were bringing in the lost. I mean lost, lost! These waves were bringing the lost up out of the lowest places of the earth. It seemed as though the sea was giving up her dead. There were pornographic stars, mass murderers, witches, many from occult and Eastern religions; souls that had committed horrendous indescribable crimes. The powers of hell were letting go of them. These last waves had the power to bring up the very bottom of the ocean.

As these waves kept coming in, the waves of salvation began covering more and more of the shore and coming upon the earth. Like a flood, the Spirit was coming in, lifting His standard upon the earth itself and multitudes were being saved as the waves of salvation continued to literally cover the earth. As these waves increased in magnitude and became humongous tidal waves, the Lord said, "*Truly as I live, all the earth shall be filled with the knowledge of the Glory of the Lord like the waters cover the sea."* Habakkuk 2:14 (KJV)

Here Come the Children

Recently, while ministering, I saw children as though they were being shot out of cannons, like cannon balls, flying into nations! I sensed the Lord saying, "There will be a proverb in the earth in the days to come: 'This is how the West was won! This is how the East was won. This is how the North and South gave up and surrendered to the kingdom of God. Balls of fire were coming out of wombs, nurseries, and children's churches!"

"But Jesus said, Suffer little children, and forbid them not, to come unto me: for of such is the kingdom of heaven." Matthew 19:4 (KJV)

"Err on

the side of

adventure."

I'm Putting Steel in Your Backbone

I sense strongly this phrase coming to me for someone reading this. "Don't play it safe. Dive in where it's over your head. Err on the side of adventure." I sense this has to do with advancing God's kingdom on earth. Jesus didn't play it safe. After Pentecost the disciples never played it safe. When persecuted they didn't pray for safety, they prayed for boldness.

The times in my life when the Lord somehow used me more was when I didn't play it safe. I jumped in without thinking it through. I had a couple confirmations but I didn't wait for three hundred. Some people thought I was crazy. Here's crazy talking to you. When you play it safe you get bored. I know what that's like.

"The master was furious. 'That's a terrible way to live! It's criminal to live cautiously like that! If you knew I was after the best, why did you do less than the least? The least you could have done would have been to invest the sum with the bankers, where at least I would have gotten a little interest." Matthew 25:26-27 (KJV)

Shaking the Gates of Hell with a Basin of Water and a Towel

In the Spirit, I saw God's foot step down into cities and regions of the earth. I knew His foot represented great authority coming.

When I saw His foot, I knew He had come to take back territory the enemy had stolen from His kingdom. As I began rejoicing at why His foot stepped down upon the earth, He interrupted my praise service with a strong command: "Wash My feet!"

I was dumbfounded. I said, "Lord, how could I ever wash your feet?"

Pastors and Leaders Washing One Another's Feet

The Lord spoke, "When you see pastors and leaders coming together and washing one another's feet, you will see My foot come down with great power, releasing whole regions and territories back into My kingdom!"

I then saw a vision of pastors and leaders humbly kneeling before each other with basins of water and towels. As they began washing one another's feet, titles, positions and even names of churches started drowning in that small basin of water. Pride, jealousy and envy were being drowned in just 12 inches of water. Weary, blistered feet that had lost their way in the dusty, soiled road of life were being healed by water and two hands of a pastor down the street. Help was never far away.

Even Our Eyes Were Being Washed with Tears

Tears began filling these basins to overflowing, tears of repentance from judging and misunderstanding one another. Even our eyes were being washed with tears to see that we were not each other's enemy, but were on the same team.

It was such a beautiful, pitiful sight. Pastors of huge churches and leaders of small churches, humbled and bowing before one another, confessing their total inability to advance God's kingdom. Revelation began breaking forth upon us of how we needed each other. Many were held in each other's grip, breaking together. Holy kisses were given out upon the faces and the feet. And a presence came as though we had kissed the Face of God.

I Saw Divine Authority Flow

At that moment, I saw divine authority flow from the feet of one who was also in our midst. A divine authority and power was being unleashed upon regions and territories. We were shaking the very gates of hell with a basin of water and a towel. It seemed the smaller we became in one another's sight, the bigger God became in the sight of the enemy. God began exalting Himself in the earth and among the heathen.

I heard the Lord speak to the angels that were present during foot washing. "Take the tears from those basins and put them in bottles. They will bring forth a great move of My Spirit to bring in the harvest."

"Be devoted to one another in love. Honor one another above yourselves." Romans 12:10 (NIV)

"Where

there's oil,

there's

spoil!"

A Vision of God's Clydesdale Horses

Note: This article was co-written by Bill and Andy Sanders. The parts that are marked with their names are their testimonies; the unmarked sections were jointly written.

Bill: I flew to New York recently on an early flight for ministry, and went to check in at a hotel at 6:45 am. The person at the counter said, "You are too early for a normal room. We are going to give you an upgraded suite and not charge any extra for it." As I stepped into the suite, the presence of the Lord was so strong that I was speechless. I am so used to doing warfare in hotel rooms to cleanse them when I enter, but I didn't need to because there was no reason for it. I said, "Lord, what is going on with this room? Nothing is in this room but You." He answered, "Someone has gone before you on this, and it's just Me and you." Since I arrived a day early, I was in His glory room all day before the meetings started. God took the heavy burden of pre-warfare away and made it extremely easy to minister that weekend.

The Clydesdales Are Coming!

"God is serious in these days about getting us help and making us whole. Where there's oil, there's spoil!"

This reminded me of the power and supernatural

ability of a Clydesdale horse. If you had access to the strength of a horse for just one day, how much more could you accomplish? How many breakthroughs would be discovered if angelic-like Clydesdales took over for you?

God is coming in power this time, and the greater the burdens and loads on the Body of Christ, the stronger the delivering power (Clydesdales) will be. These horses are so powerful that I believe they represent angelic horses in God's army. They are coming with, "Power, power, wonder-working power in the Blood of the Lamb."

Here's why they have arrived: Clydesdales are a heavy horse, a powerful breed, used for bringing major results. Commonly, Clydesdales are Scottish workhorses weighing in at around one ton. Historically, Clydesdales are also outstanding warhorses because of their height and strength. They are often more than six feet tall. In pulling power, they can normally pull around eight thousand pounds for short lengths and four hundred or so pounds for several hours a day. These superior traits mean they are able to get into certain places other horses can't because the other horses don't have the strength and stamina to do so. Also, Clydesdales are normally very calm, even in times of battle. What's interesting is that Clydesdales have been known to remain extremely docile in very loud and hostile surroundings.

"He gives strength to the weary and increases the power of the weak." (Isaiah 40:29 NIV)

You may think, "I am so weak." *"Let the weak say, 'I am strong.' Let the poor say, 'I am rich.'"* Don't count God's might out of your equation. The Lord is giving us a break in our battles of life. We can get so used to mental warfare that we need to get our minds renewed and back into the mind of Christ.

Restoration begins with "rest." Rest will become a mighty weapon in the corridors of our minds. These angelic-horses will not only pull your burdens and heavy loads, but the Lord says, "You will ride them. They will carry you, and as you rest on them they will do the work for you." I hear the Lord saying, "I'm taking over from here. Get on the Clydesdale."

Andy: On the same day Bill contacted me about the Clydesdales, just hours before, I went into an open vision where large amounts of golden oil were slowly being poured out all over the Body of Christ. At first I thought, "Wow! But, oh man...not another oil vision or dream." Oil and prophecy seem almost like cousins these days. Then I noticed what God was showing me: the oil was glistening like miniature diamonds, resting from within, as it poured down and all over millions of people and situations that they are currently walking through. The oil was filled with healing antidotes and extremely high levels of nutrients. This oil is rich in energy like honey, yet soothing like aloe. God is pouring out His best!

The Clydesdales are bringing divine, breakthrough oil! The Clydesdales are bringing relief (oil) to places where breakthrough has never been before, such as situations that have never been resolved, healings that haven't happened yet, and in some cases, family matters that have never been restored. In some situations, maybe we have never really allowed Him into certain areas of our lives in order for the Lord to completely heal us. God is bringing His oil into unpassable areas, places we have yet to discover or uncover. It is the wonderful working of God's power to set us free! God is serious in these days about getting us help and making us whole. Where there's oil, there's spoil!

God is Pouring the Oil Out and It Will:

"God is coming in power this time, and the greater the burdens and loads on the Body of Christ, the stronger the delivering power (Clydesdales) will be."

1. Bring powerful healing on the Body of Christ. The Lord is teaching us how to walk in consistent breakthroughs, and it is time to show the world that Jesus can deliver from all sins and sicknesses.

"Yet the news about Him spread all the more, so that

crowds of people came to hear Him and to be healed of their sicknesses." (Luke 5:15 NIV)

2. Supernaturally shift financial burdens off the Body of Christ. We can't doubt and walk by faith at the same time! We must trust, believe, and be very careful what we speak about money. Every time we say, "I don't have enough money," our words wrap a chain around our wallet or purse. It is time to say goodbye to debt!

"The servant's master took pity on him, canceled the debt and let him go." (Matthew 18:27 NIV)

3. Bring a fuller, greater harvest. The Clydesdales are ready to work; they are ready for action. The harvest is pushing through—it is now time to go after the lost loved ones in our families and communities!

"Don't you have a saying, 'It's still four months until harvest'? I tell you, open your eyes and look at the fields! They are ripe for harvest." (John 4:35 NIV)

Have you ever thought, whose harvest is it? It's not our harvest and even we (the laborers) are His. Everything is His! The Clydesdales (a spiritual symbol of God's help and breakthrough) will become a huge factor in bringing in the harvest. The people of the world will see the results and power of God working through us in such a way that they will chase us down to have His power (Clydesdales) and His presence (oil) in their lives. Remember, we are all a part of the harvest.

As a sign to the world and to the lost, some extremely bizarre (unfathomable) miracles are coming through oil and the topics of oil in the seasons ahead. Many miracles will be activated by releasing the healing oil over people. There will also be scientific breakthroughs in the oil industry coming soon. Remember, it isn't the oil or the Clydesdales that we worship; we worship Jesus!

Jesus said, *"For My yoke is easy and My burden is light."* Matthew 11:30 (KJV)

My Plan for Today is to Walk with Jesus

"And Enoch walked with God: and he was not; for God took him." Gen. 5:24 (KJV)

There's no mention of the great exploits or ministry which I am sure Enoch did, living 365 yrs. Nothing else is highlighted in this man's life; one who never tasted death. As they just kept walking together, they must have gotten lost in the moment of sweet communion as the Lord whispered to Enoch, "Let's take this side trail to My house. It's not far from here."

I believe the Lord missed walking with Adam in the garden. I think He misses us walking with Him each day more than anything else we could ever do for him.

"But if we walk in the light, as he is in the light, we have fellowship with one another, and the blood of Jesus, his Son, purifies us from all sin." 1 John 1:7 (NIV)

"*I saw*

heaven full

of

harvest

sickles."

"It's Party Time - Thrust Ye in the Sickle!"

In the Spirit, I saw Heaven full of harvest sickles that were destined to be used by the angels, to be thrust into the earth for a sudden reaping of the final harvest. What appeared to be the largest harvest sickle in heaven captivated the angels' attention as the Father decreed: "With one thrust of this sickle whole households will be brought into My Kingdom! Pick it up! There will be a 'thrusting' for those who are 'trusting' Me for their entire households!"

Right before the order to thrust this sickle into households, it appeared that all hell was coming against these families upon the earth - sickness, bondage and relationships that seemed impossible to ever be reconciled.

But these were the families' heaven was about to break loose upon. If all hell is coming against your household, you are right on schedule. Keep trusting for the thrusting!

I sensed the Father saying, "Before I return to the earth, you will literally see whole household salvations taking place. Mega churches have not been built large enough just for the household harvest that's about to come in! Have you noticed how many cities are building bigger stadiums this hour? Do you know why? It's not for sports. I started with Promise Keepers drawing men into stadiums to awaken them to their wives. But now I am going to awaken whole families that will need larger facilities to worship Me in."

Families Are Coming Home

Recently I was traveling with a prayer partner as we were driving past a housing development. I said to him, "Why are so many people building huge houses these days when only the husband and wife are living there? It doesn't make sense."

But I heard the Father say, "Bill, their families are coming home! Their children whom they haven't heard from or seen in years are about to come up the driveway. These houses were built for these last day family get-togethers who will experience church right in their homes. They will need a big house for some big parties; just for the prodigals that are on their way home!"

I saw angels descending with yellow gold ribbons, decorating the trees in the front yards of houses. Angels who throw parties when the lost get rescued were descending upon rooftops declaring, "It's party time! Thrust ye in the sickle!"

"By faith Noah, being warned of God of things not seen as yet, moved with fear, prepared an ark to the

saving of his house; by the which he condemned the world, and became heir of the righteousness which is by faith." Hebrews 11:7 (KJV)

The Miracle for Our Nation is in Your House!

I believe we have overlooked and underestimated the awesome power that is hidden in our families. When God created us He placed us in a family. There is something about a family atmosphere that generates the power for us to subdue the earth and bring His Kingdom into the affairs of this world. I believe satan feared the seed of the woman—for it would have the power to destroy him. He well knew that even our children would contend with him in the gate (see Psalm 127:5). I believe this is why the Lord's desire has always been to *"set the solitary (the lonely, widows, orphans and the fatherless) in families."* (Psalm 68:6).

The Greatest "National Treasure" is in Your House

In the story in 2 Kings 4, Elisha visits a widow with two sons, and she happens to have just a little oil left. Her sons were about to be taken as slaves because of the debt she owed. The government could not help her. So, she comes to Elisha for help. Elisha asked her, "What do you have in your house?" She had looked everywhere for her answer except in her own house. In other words, Elisha was saying to her, "You don't know the awesome miracle power that is in your own house!"

I believe today many are looking to see what is in the White House that will save our nation. But God is asking His people this hour, "What is in your house? Do you realize the greatest 'national treasure' is in your own house?" I believe that great "national treasure" lies within our family members. Many times, diamonds in the rough are hard to see. The troubles that have come into your family are about to bless you!

"I'm Equipping Families to Take Their Nations!"

Joshua 24:15 "...*As for me and my house, we will serve the Lord!*

I believe as Joshua was declaring to the nation of Israel to choose life or death, he was proclaiming the importance of not only his personal choice, but also his heart for his family.

Joshua's heart for every father and mother was for them to decree that their families would serve the Lord, also. Was he sensing the power that families hold in influencing the whole nation from being destroyed? I sense he believed that if God could save him, God could save his family. And I further sense that he was believing if God could save his family, He could also save the whole nation! He believed that the "national treasure" was in his house!

Acts 16:31 *"Believe on the Lord Jesus Christ, and thou shalt be saved, and thy house."*

I sense that we need to decree now more than ever that our whole household shall be saved, and begin to decree over America: "One Nation, Our Nation, Under God!" Our Father still has this dream in His heart, that not only your family, but a whole nation can be saved in a day!

Isaiah 66:8 *"Who has heard such a thing? Who has seen such things? Shall the earth be made to bring forth in one day? Or shall a nation be born at once? For as soon as Zion travailed, she brought forth her children."*

Could it be, ever since the garden of Eden, that the enemy well knows that families hold the hidden power to destroy his kingdom and deliver whole nations? Is it any wonder that he unleashes hell upon families?

Joel 2:28 (KJV) *"And it shall come to pass afterward that I will pour out My Spirit on all flesh; your sons and your daughters shall prophesy, your old men shall dream dreams, your young men shall see visions."*

I believe this great outpouring was intended for our families first, and then God knew nothing else could stop it from going upon all flesh! I even sense that each family member has certain keys for the family's health and deliverance that could ultimately result in the deliverance for our nation. Look again. I believe the answer for our nation is right inside of our own house!

"O America, May I Blow My Breath into Your Households?"

" I want to blow My breath into the nostrils of every family member. Great-grandparents down to the babies in the womb. I am about to make personal house calls in this nation. I am coming 3-D Technicolor straight to where you live. There are angels standing at attention with your personal addresses written on them that will be released to set up camp round about your dwelling place, to deliver family members far and near. Houses will be turned into homes.

"May I blow My breath into your households? Prodigals will phone home. Missing children unable to be found for many years will be rescued by the breath of My Spirit! I have been patient in the past with your family members who have resisted Me. I have gently knocked on the door of their house and hearts. But now I will huff and puff and blow the front door down! I'm coming in!"

The Miracle for Our Nation is in your House!

I believe God's own shofar is beginning to blow into our households right now, releasing the sounds of salvation, healing, deliverance and the equipping of whole families to take their nations! Receive it now.

Prayer: "Lord, we receive Your breath of life into our families' nostrils to live again. We call each family member a royal priesthood, a chosen generation. We call those things that are not as though they already are. We call them saved, healed and delivered. We call them our 'National Treasures'! We are going to accept our family members right where they are and love them unconditionally. We are going to treat them as though they are already saved.

"As for me and my house, we will serve the Lord!" Joshua 24:15 (KJV)

It's Time to Hang Out Your Shingle

To 'hang out your shingle' means to begin working as a professional from your own office. A shingle is a small sign board that you put out to the public so that they can see it and know what you are available to do.

It's Time to Allow Yourself and Your Gift to be Made Known

Concerning the servant who buried his gift or talent in the ground. Matthew 25:26 (Message Bible) "*The master was furious. That's a terrible way to live! It's criminal to live cautiously like that! The least you could have done would have been to invest the sum with the bankers, where at least I would have gotten a little interest. Take it and give it to the one who risked the most. And get rid of this 'play-it-safe' who won't go out on a limb. Throw him out into utter darkness!*"

I sense the Lord saying, "It's time to allow yourself to be made known and come forth with the gifts and the talents that I have deposited inside of you for such a time as this. I have need of you. Your gifts are not for yourself, they are for others." Don't be so humble that you think if you put yourself out there and let yourself be known for what God has put in you that that would be prideful. That is nothing by false humility! Romans 12:13 (NIV) says, *"Do not think of yourself more highly than you ought."* The downside of this verse is that often too many of us think of ourselves too lowly than we ought to think.

Remember we are in Christ and Christ is in us. We are not lifting up ourselves but we are lifting Him up so He can draw all men unto Himself. When we hide our gifts and talents, we often hide or bury ourselves with them. 2 Timothy 1:6 (KJV) *"Neglect not the gift that is in you."* I believe Paul was saying to Timothy, "Stir up your gift and make it available to others."

Many Will Discover Businesses and Entrepreneurships Being Birthed in Their Own Homes

The gift of 'helps' is always having the desire and ability to help others. I believe if we have the desire God will see to it that the ability will be there. I believe the gift of 'helps' of wanting to help people will be the womb where creativity and revelation will conceive to birth many businesses and services that have been unheard of until now.

Go Out On a Limb and 'Hang Your Shingle Out' There... Out On a Limb is Where the Fruit Grows!

Many who lost their jobs thinking they couldn't exist without it will find themselves self- employed and working for a King! When Jesus said, "I must be about My father's business,' I believe He was referring to meeting the practical needs of people as well as their spiritual needs. All work, whatever we think is secular or spiritual is the same to the Lord. It is all His business.

Go ahead. Hang out your shingle!

"Each of you should use whatever gift you have received to serve others, as faithful stewards of God's grace in its various forms." 1 Peter 4:10 (NIV)

"Let my babies go!"

I Saw Angelic Midwives Interrupting the Spirit of Abortion

Prayers seemed to have mounted up and taken wings ascending to the throne room, crying out on behalf of the unborn. I heard many angels conversing, "We just got a breakthrough assignment to deliver the unborn! Tell them to keep crying out and pleading the Blood of Jesus...the spirit of abortion is beginning to be notified, 'Let My Babies Go!'"

'Angelic' Midwives Are Being Assigned to Hand Deliver the Deliverers

It seemed like a season equivalent to when God had called Moses, in his mother's womb, to be a deliverer to the nation of Israel. In Moses' time Pharaoh sent a decree to destroy every male child being born. But the fear of God came upon the midwives and they saved those babies.

Moses was one of them that was delivered. These kind of 'hand delivered' babies deliver nations!

I sense once again we are in a season of intervention where the fear of God is beginning to fall on abortion clinics, as 'angelic' midwives are now being assigned to doctors and nurse practitioners.

A stronger cry from the throne became even louder for intercession as an angel began proclaiming, "I think we got another Moses here! Another David, another Deborah, and, yes, there is another Esther coming out of that womb! Keep prayer coming up. . . these babies have an anointing for the nations!"

'You Are Not Carrying a Mistake; You Are Carrying a Miracle'

I saw the Holy Spirit overshadowing many mothers who, like Mary, were overwhelmed with what to think and to do next as they were surprised by their pregnancy. But the Holy Spirit began to melt their hearts, as it was revealed by God, Himself, "Fear not, that holy thing which shall be born of thee is of Me. You are not carrying a mistake; you are carrying a miracle!"

I saw in the Spirit many babies being offered up for adoption. God had already handpicked married couples and placed His desire in their hearts to extend their families. These children appeared as arrows in their quivers who would eventually speak with the enemies in the gates of their cities and nations!

"Babies unplanned are Heaven's surprises; unplanned by man for satan's demises!"

"Lo, children are a heritage of the LORD: and the fruit of the womb is his reward." Psalm 127:3 (KJV)

"Oh America, Is That a Tear in Your Eye?"

In the Spirit I saw hairline cracks appearing on the marble floor of the White House. As I saw these hairline cracks, I sensed the Lord speaking, *"For there is hope of a tree, if it be cut down, that it will sprout again, and that the tender branch (of government) thereof will not cease. Though the root thereof wax old in the earth, and the stock thereof die in the ground; Yet through the scent of water it will bud, and bring forth boughs like a plant."* Job 14:7-9 (KJV)

I sensed the Lord saying, "As Samson's hair began to grow again, so are the spiritual roots of this nation." As I saw the cracking of the floor increase, it was like the very foundation of deception and greed was beginning to be dismantled...exposing the enemy! (The enemy is not a man, but satan.)

I said to the Lord, "What has caused these spiritual roots to begin to grow again at this time?" I sensed the Father saying, "I have collected in a bottle every tear that swelled up in every eye that has mourned for this nation. These tears in My bottle are now being poured out over America, causing her roots of righteousness to begin to spring forth in the land."

Paramedic Angels

In the spirit, I saw what appeared to be "paramedic angels" dispatched, dropping from the heavens, as in parachutes, landing on the front lawn of the White House. It seemed that those grass roots of righteousness that began to crack the White House floor had set off an alarm in Hell, summoning these angels with urgency to surround the White House.

I saw multitudes of other angels descending upon and filling up the mall of the nation's capitol. I saw that these angels had the scripture written all over them, *"If My people who are called by My name shall humble themselves and seek My face, and turn from their wicked ways; then will I hear from Heaven and will forgive their sin and heal their land."* 2 Chronicles 7:14 (KJV)

Warring on Corporate Prayer

These Second Chronicles angels seemed to have had assignments throughout the ages to descend upon nations that were in critical time frames where a nation seemed to be hanging in the balance of going either way. These angels warred solely and strictly on "corporate prayer" only! I sensed they had come to Washington, DC, but now were given orders to wait on the rising tide of "corporate prayer" from the heart of America.

Certain angels were released into war for a nation only through tears...nothing else moved these ones. I asked the Lord, "Father, why 'paramedic angels'? I have never heard of them."

I sensed He responded, "I plan to give mouth to mouth resuscitation to America and kiss her face again!"

"Who has ever heard of such things? Who has ever seen things like this? Can a country be born in a day or a nation be brought forth in a moment? Yet no sooner is Zion in labor than she gives birth to her children." Isaiah 66:8 (NIV)

Shofars Are Being Summoned into Battle ... To Blow Life into the Nations!

**About the Shofar: The shofar is a ceremonial ram's horn (trumpet) of ancient Israel. The shofar holds a prominent role in the history of Israel. The ram's horn is identified with the ram that became the substitute sacrifice for Isaac in Genesis 22:1-19. The ram typified the future sacrifice that Jesus would become for us.

Is the Shofar Still Effective?

Yes! Our battles today are with principalities and

powers of darkness, but they are still battles! *"And the three hundred (of Gideon's army) blew the trumpets (shofars), and the Lord set every man's sword against his fellow, even throughout all the host (of the enemy): and the host fled to Bethshittah in Zererath, and to the border of Abelmeholah, unto Tabbath."* Judges 7:22

I Wouldn't Have Chosen That Weapon

God is still calling forth the foolish things to use for His glory. If He can use you and me, He can use anything -- and get away with it!

Most victories in times of war in the Old Testament came through unusual weapons ordered by the Lord. Samson with the jawbone of an ass slew a thousand Philistines! Israel marched around a city and took it with a shout! Jehoshaphat's army was outnumbered like the sands of the seashore and He was led to put his loudest mouth singers on the very front line of battle. They began to sing praises as they marched into the enemy camp and God sent ambushes against the enemy to confuse them; and all the enemies were dead when the hymn-sing was over! They didn't even get to fight in this battle!

I have been to an army base in Israel, recently. Their army still sings during their training drills... devil beware! I must confess, if I was commanding these armies, "I wouldn't have chosen these weapons . . .

but God did!"

The Shofar Blows Confusion into The Camp of the Enemy

I believe the most terrifying sound in the enemy's ears is the sound of the shofar! Every time a shofar blows, the devil doesn't know whether it's one of us or Gabriel himself blowing that last trump of God! When shofars are blown, they blow confusion into the enemy's camp -- every time!

I believe one of the reasons the Lord is calling forth the weapon of the shofar this hour is to send confusion into the camp of the terrorists! I sense great fear and the terror of the Lord will be released upon them through this mighty, foolish weapon!

When Gideon Blew His . . . I Blew Mine!

As I read how the Spirit of the Lord came upon Gideon and he blew a trumpet (shofar), I asked the Lord, "When the Spirit came upon Gideon and he blew a shofar, was that Gideon blowing or was that you?"

The Lord answered, "When Gideon blew his . . . I blew Mine!"

Many Jewish people believe that the trump of God in Heaven is not a Louis Armstrong-type trumpet, but a shofar (a ram's horn -- or His could be called a lamb's horn).

I heard of the testimony of a man who died and went to heaven. He said he saw the shofar of God there. He said, "It is fifteen miles long!" When it is blown it will literally raise the dead down through every generation of time who believe in Jesus Christ the Messiah! I believe the Lord is raising up shofars in this hour, getting us used to hearing their sound; for when Gabriel blows the Shofar of God, it will be the last sound out of here!

When a Weapon is Loaded, it Goes Off Every Time

In 1995, I was invited to blow the shofar at an International Aglow Conference in Long Beach, California. Blowing the shofar was new to me. Before the conference in the hotel room, I thought I better practice blowing it. At the very first blow, in the Spirit I saw angels descending upon Long Beach and the whole region! I sensed the Lord saying, "Be careful, this baby is loaded! There is no need to practice with this weapon!"

I have learned that when a shofar is blown, it calls forth angelic armies into that region to fight against the powers of darkness, to take back that territory into God's kingdom! When I blew the shofar at the conference, into nine thousand people, and had them shout the walls down inside of their households, divorces were cancelled, marriages were restored and even reports came in of missing children being found!

All I Know is God Said, "Blow!"

I wonder how God might organize a mass blowing of shofars from those who know they are called to blow one. I sense there are many who think that to blow a shofar isn't for them. Let me ask you a question... how do you know unless you blow one?

I used to think only certain people are called to blow the shofar. But I honestly am not sure anymore. I think anyone can pull the trigger of a loaded weapon, even a little child! I will let that decision of blowing one be between you and the Lord.

When the Lord first called me to blow the shofar, He made one thing clear: "Bill, when you blow it, it will be Me blowing, because I live in you! By faith, I believe when I blow into one end of the shofar, the very breath of God comes out the other -- because He lives in me! It's all by faith that God is calling forth these foolish weapons again, this hour, in time of war!

I sense the Lord would have us to personally be led by Him when and where to blow in this season of war. I believe a good place to start is right at home. Let's blow the confusion out of our own lives and families! And let the Lord lead you from there! You can stand right where you are and blow into a nation. There is no distance with the breath of God! He will lead us. Check in with Him for the details . . . all I know is God said, "Blow!"

"Blow the trumpet in Zion; sound the alarm on my holy hill. Let all who live in the land tremble, for the day of the LORD is coming. It is close at hand-" Joel 2:1 (NIV)

"Begin

to lift

the veils

of

singleness..."

End-Time Weddings

I sensed that not only was the Father excited over His Own Son's wedding that would soon take place, but He was seemingly beside Himself for the joy of a multitude of long awaited "end-time" weddings that would take place upon the earth, just preceding the greatest wedding in the Universe.

"Get those six water pots out again and fill them with 'living' water! I've saved the very best wine for last, for these end-time weddings."

I saw veils of singleness that had been covering many single men and women for years, in spite of their desire to marry. These veils were actually covering them to protect and hide them from wrong relationships. Many had thought, "What's wrong with me? No one seems to notice me or even look at me."

But I saw the wisdom of God hard at work to preserve these chosen ones for the person whom the Lord was preparing and keeping separate for them. I sensed the Father saying to their guardian angels, "Begin to lift the veils of 'singleness' off of their faces. It's time for them to see and be seen by the ones whom I have ordained for them. As I sent an angel to direct the footsteps of Isaac's servant to find Rebecca for him, I am sending angels before them to guide them."

Veils were coming off of many "widows and widowers" as the Lord was proclaiming, "Your lonely days are coming to an end!"

I saw divorce papers being shredded as some who had divorced each other were now making plans to renew their wedding vows and start over!

All of Heaven seemed to be ecstatic over earthly weddings. To them, each wedding brings heaven and earth a little closer, with the intent to portray the ultimate marriage that all creation awaits...the marriage supper of the Lamb!

"He will send his angel ahead of you, and he will see to it that you find a wife there for my son." Genesis 24:7 (NLT)

Contact the Author

Bill Yount
Blowing the Shofar Ministries
132 E. North Ave.
Hagerstown, MD 21740
E-mail: theshofarhasblown@juno.com
www.billyount.com

Sign up for Bill's prophetic email list at:
www.billyountweekly.com

If you would like to be blessed by the ministry of Bill Yount, please contact him at the above e-mail address. He is available to minister at your church, conference, meeting, coffee house or anyplace God's people are gathered in His Name.

Other books by Bill Yount are available at Amazon.com:

The Power of Real / Transparent Prophetic Encouragement

Some Hear Thunder... I Hear A Roar! / Supernatural Encounters & Stories to Encourage Your Heart

I Heard Heaven Proclaim / Prophetic Words of Encouragement

Prophetic Stones of Remembrance / A Legacy for the End Times

Made in USA - Kendallville, IN
1188529_9781724516336
10.30.2020 1558